CALIFORNIA
and
NEW MEXICO

CALIFORNIA and NEW MEXICO

22 Poems
by
Webster Young

with Photography by
John Axline

EDITIONS D'AUTEURS

RESOURCE *Publications* • Eugene, Oregon

CALIFORNIA AND NEW MEXICO
22 Poems

Copyright © 2020 Webster Young. All rights reserved. Except for brief quotations in critical publications or reviews, no part of this book may be reproduced in any manner without prior written permission from the publisher. Write: Permissions, Wipf and Stock Publishers, 199 W. 8th Ave., Suite 3, Eugene, OR 97401.

Resource Publications
An Imprint of Wipf and Stock Publishers
199 W. 8th Ave., Suite 3
Eugene, OR 97401

www.wipfandstock.com

PAPERBACK ISBN: 978-1-7252-6181-5
HARDCOVER ISBN: 978-1-7252-6182-2
EBOOK ISBN: 978-1-7252-6183-9

Manufactured in the U.S.A.   01/17/20

§ THE BAY AT NIGHT

San Francisco -
lime green
gold and carmine,
ruby reds
streetcar sign
orange light
green-blue-white, intense
across the bay at night
a spray of diamonds,
tiny stars
in graphite powder
stretched along the dim horizon's
silhouette of mounding hills
ghostly, reclining,
a sleeping princess --
signaling jewels
spilled from a casket,
strewn on the bay
from a giant basket.

A worldly city
lives as a vision, a tale, a Psalm...
We watched from the roof in the Mars-black night:
our New Jerusalem, not descending -
there across a depth of bay,
the waxing and waning gods
in her lights at play.

§ THE GOLDEN GATE

Golden days lying back on lawns
beside the dorm
looking off the hill and there
across the big blue bay
the golden gate
the bridge, the reddish span,
crossing from and filling in
between two lands -
Presidio to south Marin.

Every day the sun came down,
setting through the bridge
and burned to red
and turned to gold,
and lowered into sea.

We Berkeley students knew -
no postcard this, no travel ad,
but all reality -
the gate was real,
gold was to be had.
Right out there - beyond the gate,
down and to the left of big mount Tam,

the globe had called,
the ultra blue above
the aqua blue below
California waters
streaked in clouds

that wisped above the sun
and melted all to marble
telling us by day
of each new marvel.

Some were early,
some were late,
but last or first,
the same reward
was held for them
that looked upon the gate.

And in that year I then so early
passed on through the golden door,
the bridge to every gift
that ever waits.

The one as great,
as all-Pacific,
more than all the seas,
the one beyond the gate,
had called me first,
at age eighteen,
and in the morning
made me walk.
And North I went,
to Concord, Davis, Sacramento.
from age eighteen,
the California sacred fields
became the land
where I was born,
again where I was born.

§ STEINBECK COUNTRY

That California is a land of gold,
is what the poppies told -
a land that bears in air
the old Franciscan prayers.
They fly Sierra skies,
filtering down to all
to Pilon, Lenny, Doc, Tom Joad
who sought a prize from life
living in the valley

from old Franciscan prayers -
coming down to bless the crops,
of San Joaquin and Sacramento
singing love that never stops -
of Carmel, Solvang, Monterey,
tomato, prune, and vineyard grape,
almond tree and pear.

Before the aquaduct was made,
when Jeffers lived in Pasadena,
before the time of Chavez,
cottages in rows were set,
with simple rooms of pine and board.
They stand today
on outskirts of the towns -
and still they house the Okie,
the worker and the poor.
for Everyman -

their single windows looking out
to valley floors of straw and golden tan

§ OF MICE AND MEN
(In Memoriam Kenneth Frantz)

Lenny, Lenny
could not make it -
you did not reach
what others do.
Reaching out,
you tore the dress,
and then the court
refused redress...

And yet you lived
in sunny orchards
worked in clutch of vibrant color
Van Gogh free,
on Steinbeck porches
propped in hills of golden straw,
and deep green oaks - Provence.
You painted raw
those halos haunting faces,
father, mother,
ancestry,
couched in fine geometry.

Lenny, Lenny...
missions ended with you.
Paintings sit there stack to stack...
and memory goes back.

Did Lenny know,
in leaving Weed for Monterey,

how life would go - and founder?

Now Kenneth Frantz has died unknown,
and sometimes wind that blows upon
the mounding Coast Range hills,
a hint of spirit spills...

What of Steinbeck, what of Joad?
What of mysteries in paint,
that wait, their tales to unload?

SAN FRANCISCO

Presidio and fields.
Bands are playing parties.

Cliff House on grey days -
Pacific waves below,
they crossed from China,
Today they rip the stones;
tomorrow they will turn, in placid times
in mild sun, to reach in crescents
misty Half Moon Bay.
The Legion of Honor in whitewashed stone -
classic line - is not so far a drive away
past cypresses and eucalyptus,
and coastal pines.
But...turn back East
and drive the dips and hills
to Scott Street, the Marina,
we'll pass the painted ladies,
canary yellow, decked in stripes
Victorian, of sunset orange,
planes of white, and turquoise blue -
the shelters of the Renaissance -
Ferlinghetti,
Jeffers, poets -
Rexroth, Brother Antoninus,
painters of the bay,
the figurative movement of the post war days
of David Park and Clifford Still

and Diebenkorn,
and Kenneth Frantz unknown.

Or drive the full way East
by rolling down with cable cars
and end up on the wharf,
where London sat
at cafes near the docks
and wrote his rhymes
in time before the earthquake shocks
that brought the city almost flat.

For all that trial
the city built back well.
The Francis Drake hotel,
the San Francisco Opera,
the modern churches,
the missions as of old.

and after stood to foster
Steinbeck as a writer,
youthful Ansel Adams
charities of Randolph Hearst -

this Gold Coast of the wandering free,
who came to find a freedom
in the fog town by the sea.

MUIR WOODS

We from the class
at Berkeley,
would drive and find Marin,
and turn in west,
to pastures and a lake along the road,
our holy quest:
the monument - Muir Woods.

And there you'd walk
where trunks like giant rooted columns,
rise to heights to block the sky,
and awe the paths and forest,
and cast a calming shade
on the low creek ebbing by.

Smaller stands form circles,
holy campers' enclaves,
and some Sequoias, there since Christ,
disseminate a peace,
that comes to every walker,
a grace,
of spirit, nature, time, and space.

The creek flows perfect
on and over rocks and pebbles in its sand.
And by this creek the Miwoks
stood and told their stories of the land:

"Once, in a pool of the creek
a certain rock was placed by God

down below the stream,
below the flow of time -
and Black Crow, Miwok Saint,
had seen the rock make time slow down -
and all the people walking by,
moving almost timelessly,
he saw them
gliding almost listlessly
perceived them
walking in Eternity."

§ BIG SUR, CALIFORNIA
New Camaldoli Hermitage at Night

The sea thought it was all,
the gamboling
lucent,
gentle blue Pacific -
until it met the shadowed rock immovable
headland's massive shoulders
the granite bulk of continent
the bending hulk of coastland
birth of earth,
mass of land
tabling life, this place, and man.

On this, the many stars and moon above
cast light on beach and breakers.

The waves incessant
rhyme upon the rocks and strands
pound against the coastal lands,
beat to silk the whitened sands
and roll a voice that rises high
to huts that stand on cliffs
and look out to the moon, sea, and sky.

Fields of bay, of sage and brush
that deck the cliffs and mountain flanks
amplify the cricket craze,
carried on the breeze
that climbs the angled banks
in scents of herbs and salt and seas.

From high,
the sea is like a floor
and moonlight shines a path
to far eternal distant doors.

The monastery bell -
sounds in a cosmic drone
a metal knell
that shakes and wakes,
reverberates,
and vibrates all to belly and bones.

Get up and see out past the dark!
lean out from these cliffs
and touch eternal place,
pregnant as the sea.
and turn your heart
in single action simple
to where you always had to be:
the source and grandeur's place.

§ THE CAREER of ANSEL ADAMS

Music, nature- both have a claim
to the self-same fundamental,
the gold proportion's
underlying song:
And nature played a chord
for youthful Ansel Adams -
piano was his love and law.

In practice at piano
he reveled in the melody
of great composers' work
determined that their music be
his life vocation.

But taking up the walking staff
to hike Yosemite
he made his early photographs,
He brought on burros
camera, tripod, plates, and lens
and captured stone in black and white
and found divinity,
wholeness, self,
in clear transcendant light.

Yet still he loved the sounds of strings
the grand piano soundboard,
his music still ascendant.
He labored in the city
studied all musical works for piano -

his goal was virtuosity.
And on the side he worked at his photography.

In music's quest he found he could not marry -
Life in music is far too cruel,
for those who need stability.
He tired soon of struggle
tired of musician trouble
tautness in ambition's rope
finally broke.

Scents of pines, Sierra valleys called
and made him leave it all -
and down he fled
to Fresno and Yosemite
and married one he feared to marry
and to the mountain rocks and glens
he turned his camera lens again.

Another kind of music,
another kind of beauty
answered to his need
for harmony,
and now the mass of mountain might
in tones of grey and black would utter
all he tried to capture
with snap of shutter and photo plate.

He'd walk in long to mountain rocks,
returning to the darkroom,
and in his hands the photo print

became another sounding board.

He made the sound just right
and captured tones in nature -
those within Sierra light
the contrast found in clouds
the cuts and rifts and pines,
of inland valley fjords -
Half Dome lines, the white of falls,
the jagged rock in chiaroscuro -
Zion's walls.

And this was also music's might
Brahms's light,
the massive symphony.

And soon the prints of Ansel Adams,
became a nation's emblems -
a nation that would strain
to find relations to retain
the balance of technology
and nature.
With music too,
with Muzak all around,
his country knew no pastorale,
no chord of nature
singing its polyphony.

Adams quit piano
to pioneer photography
and in his country
technology and harmony
are still a picture half developed.

§ MANY MANSIONS

Of those valleys,
triangular escarpments,
upper fields, past the tree line,
inclines, canyons, slopes and foothills,
ridges, gorges, dry creeks, flood plains,
creek beds, pools, and stony rills,
- seen upon that range of mountains -
one can only really know a few.

In my Father's house...

The many hundred places -
trails, passes, shoulders, saddles,
notches, hilltops, boulders, bedrock,
outcrops, cliff walls,
forests, clearings -
even in that range,
across from you in view -
too many for a lifetime,
to really understand.

... are many mansions.

Just standing on one ridge,
with views across the knolls
a thousand pines,
ten thousand
evergreens,
one hundred thousand,

stretch from mountain ridges on.
And in the world,
one tree for each who ever lived -
as if they all were souls.

...I go prepare a place for you.

THE CALIFORNIA AQUADUCT

If you drive I-5
from Sacramento south
you parallel the aquaduct.
But go in March and start at Redding
to see the Sacramento-San Joaquin
blooming in the early spring.

The almonds trees and apples
have sprouted rose and pinks
and drop their petals
bedding orchard floors
and anyone who thinks
that California isn't heaven
should drive to see the valleys come alive.

The petals make their carpets,
linking acre square to acre
underneath the branches
joining quilts that blanket
more and more of what you see
of orchard, farm, and valley.
You think it can't go on,
but passing over ridges
looking down to fields,
miles and miles of cherry pinks
stretch far down to many counties.
right and left, in fields,
branches, vines, and roots
healthy in the springtime air

call you to their mauve and cherry lairs.

So all of California dresses in the early spring,
a debutante in silken white and pink,
rustling. The valley earth is overturned
and growing things, in little shoots
have thrown away in March
the damp and deadening winter.
And when you come to Stockton
as much in bloom, as much in tune
with spring throughout the valley
as any city on the route,
a little farther on
you take the time to stop,
and find that you have company.

Another road cuts through the land,
but this one placid, bland, and suave,
with banks of concrete-white
its traveller blue and shimmering -
the water flowing south
to give its life to all the land.

The California aquaduct
links in glimmering skein
Turlock, Tracy,
Avenal and Banos.
It passes the Sierra chain,
cradled by the coastal range,
crosses the Tehachapis,
to Palmdale and the southern state.

and passes every university -
the California unities,
the chain of missions
in all the valley north to south
cerulean as its waters rush
to make the land between the mountains
blush.

§ MISSION SAN JUAN CAPISTRANO

Beneath the Orange County sky
where scents fly of ocean,
walls of whitewashed stucco,
ruins of the stucco walls,
hold the iron mission bells
of San Juan Capistrano,
acropolis Americano.

Just outside the walls
across the way
are cafes, shops, and mini-malls
done in style Hispano.
And going in the gate
you pay admission,
to see the thirty rose beds,
multicolored bowers,
where coastal breeze refreshes olive trees
and cypresses
that shade the benches under walls.

Plazas stand surrounded in their
terracotta serenata,
lined by arches, old arcades,
that once housed all the trades
from casting lead, or parrafin,
to making bread.

Around the whole are Indian graves,
the tribe of Gabrieleno,

They lived in peace,
with no revolt
and never reconquista
as happened in New Mexico.

The American acropolis
was once a heliopolis
where sun shone down on irrigation
Gabrielenos worked in fields
and tilled the mission terra
between the day's oblations.
and all of them would share the yield
in great communal meals.

Father Serra
reached his goal
a commune Gabrieleno,
Mexicano,
in tune, an earthen altar
a living psalter
Christiano.

§ MISSION SAN FERNANDO REY

San Fernando Rey
sits within an angle
bordered by the freeway -
and looking at the map,
you'd think the road would strangle
peace where people came to pray.

And yet the angled park
where mission buildings sit
is many acres large
and paths go every way -
No noise of cars -
yes, peace can still be found
near the palms and pines
inhabiting those grounds -
hidden from the multitude
speeding by
in numbers hard to measure.

Along the lawns and walkways
you'll reach the storied chapel
altar standing high
deserving of its fame,
multi-levels
bathed in gold
housing saints
and San Fernando -
saintly King of of Spain.

A little landscaped garden

nestled by a building wall
is crammed with flowers
a grave is circled by path
a stellar name of Hollywood
whose wife would have him buried there
to lie down with the good.

In old adobe stalls
of more historic structures
the rooms become
a gift shop and museum -
with photos on the walls...

and there you see one black and white -
three feet wide and two foot tall,
dating from the 1800's:
the older Valley -
captured from Granada Hills,
a panorama shot of all.

You see the valley floor
from Calabasas
a nearly endless plain to Eastern hills.
For mile on empty mile,
not one road, one house, or train,
no man -
a nearly virgin California land.

And in the whole
one speck is what you see:

the old Franciscan mission

alone
in that inland sea
of field and flower
the outpost of the Friars who prayed
so fervently with locals,
for what would come to be.

And now it sits within an angle,
where freeways cut and slice,
but all those prayers are still the Angelus,
the Angeles,
a guardian angel
of California paradise.

§ MISSION SAN GABRIEL

Not so far from Griffith Park,
east and south some miles,
below the great San Gabriels -
and near the grounds botanical,
of Huntington's estates,
is a neighborhood where sits the place
that pre-dates Pasadena
Hollywood,
and every road and deed of land,
and gave its name
to the mountains there
that stand and block the north horizon -
the mission of the robed Franciscans -
San Gabriel.

The native tribe
who lived upon the lands
from coast to far inland,
who worked within the mission,
was called the Gabrieleno.

They're buried there
around the walls of stucco white
amid the palm and cypress.
and peace has settled on this place

so close to Pasadena.
A choir's in the Spanish chapel,
high school students,
singing music for the mass

by Palestrina.
music so angelic
even Bach had called it master.

So close to Pasadena,
humble buildings built with vigas:
sheltered from the hurried pace
of number 10 or 605.
and countless cars
that crawl or race
their ways to east and west
and pass by
Pasadena.

§ THE KINGDOM

Decades ago,
because I was poor,
and still I had Hope,
and while I was young,
it was the Kingdom.

The towns and the fields,
of old Yolo County,
the humble state road
the grey sky archangel -
living forever.

Soon it was written,
and now I remember,
was all this the Kingdom
now resurrected?

Friends at my door -
would talk for an hour.
I'd take my blue coat,
and walk and debate on the world,
of things and ideas that would flower.

The simple white cottage,
the Doc and pisanos,
the upright piano,
and we poor in spirit
at something eternal

and I almost wise
  and Doc was the greatest
  of men in my eyes.
  But still I would go -
  I went away -
  to find out my part
  in the arts of the cities.

  Now Doc is gone
  and some things have changed,
  but old Yolo County,
  is ever the same.

  Detail in blessings
  is still recollected

  but was this the Kingdom
  hidden in things
  now resurrected?

NEW MEXICO

§ THE MOST GLORIOUS SUNSET
(A Saint's Passing)

The most glorious sunset
is where the Light
lays down in complex clouds
that almost blocked His rays,
but as he sets
they, edged with fire
become a world, an
archipelago burned to red,
a land of myriad yellow islands,
paradisiacal dreams
of what might be, and could have been.

And people look in wonder
at the passing
of one who shed his blessing
on all those clouds
that blocked his light
and now they all turn grey --
his body sinks
below the lines of
hillocks and horizons
and leaves the world -
burning.

.§ LOW ON WATER (Cerrillos, New Mexico)

Even in these desert lands,
naked earth, dry and pink,
where pumice powder makes a soil
fluffy batter, rising with soda
when soaked in winter waters,
and where in summer, much the same
it dries out light and cakes
and seems to take the air,
when August's latter days burn bright
almost white, and day becomes too hot,
and walking I begin to bend
with desolation riding on my shoulder,

then sometimes looking down to tufts
of grass and crackled ground,
I'll see a tiny yellow flower,
and cheered by evidence of gold,
the softness of a petal,
reminded of the health and light,
the butter color's power,
still walk on amidst the tan
and tawn of parched earth, and now look up
and down the road, consoled, and yet
still wonder. Where is water,
the element of aqua? Though it rained
but one day past, the burdened air
can filter through in one long blast
and water is the thing that I most lack.

§ ASPENS AT BIG TESUQUE

At campgrounds
named for Big Tesuque creek,
you take the trail ascending,
going up the stream.
The perfect water
washes orange stones
and speaks aloud of nature
left without a human touch.

And standing by the path,
are crowds of quaking Aspen
blanketing the mountain flanks,
carpets of one kind of tree,
on massive ridges standing out
to west and south,
Aspens growing wide and free.

They're near to you -
a choir of harps,
their trunks are strings of white -
making up their octaves
telling their angles set in light.

And some faint hand,
a message in the shadows.
plays those harps
that vibrate near within your sight.

Their barks are full of eyes,
and every trunk will look at you

and tell you he is wise.
They striate back in depth,
and seem to play a game,
They want to be a painting
of the Painter's artifice
building its own frame.

§ THE END OF DAYS

The sun beams far and lends his light
to long lanes and flat planes
in yellowed rays abutting on the mountain chain.

Across the central desert floor
cottage sides and humble fields,
parallelograms and diamonds flat,
are lit receivers of the rays
and all become a checkerboard.

From East to West, straight through, a line:
the rail path of glowing track. Its narrow iron
melds with earth and points to where the orb of fire
sets and makes the track an orange wire.

The elements are held in thrall and even-ness is all.
The rays have reached to flatest flat,
stopping for a time of peace -
the end of days - light across the plain.

§ SUNRISE

Before you see the sun
you see his light.
Before you see the truth
you see a sign -
a glow of his approach
or our approach -
the Earth revolves to him.

Before you see the orb
you see the rose
colors herald power's closeness
the courtiers of his realm announce
his greatness as he goes.

The whiter lights of night,
are dimmed by him and soon go out.
The perfect ray,
the shining shaft
purely grows,
on time, on plan,
and smiles on man,
attending on his theater.

And then the real rises
over the horizon.
Full out the yellow fire
brings to sight
material life -
now many times more real
when shown in light.

The stage already there
was shrouded in the dark of night,
The earth was waiting,
dark was on the harbor
holding boats
huddled where they float.

The yellow lights have hit the boards,
Now, actors, go in zeal
realize the play.
The light of life
has stark revealed
matter of the real.

§ THE BLUEBIRD OF HAPPINESS

The bird weighs lightly,
stopping any place -
Pinon boughs and branches,
Juniper, greying sheds that look across
from ridge to desert valley

To him the least is great.
A sunbeam on a window cheers
a memory is big and he is small -
the world is great.

The view is panoramic
and from his krall of Pinon greens
his feathers make a deeper shade
of blue cascade,
cool and rich,
and more than streams,
adds a note of blue cadet
to all, to cap the whole,
And he is small - the world is great.

Streams of topaz blue that feed the well,
flow through land and air.
He flits off far and high,
follows fancy,
tiny eye on canyons
cut horizon to horizon,
and he is small
within the growing sky.

§ DECEMBER SUN IN AN UNFAMILIAR PLACE

The glory of the Advent sun
white upon
the burnished plain
and metal roofed adobes:

"Rejoice right now..."
Whatever state you're in,
stop for joy.
Whatever's still potential,
It will be.
Whatever has been realized,
it is won.
The shock of change
is still to come -
when ending meets beginning,
when solstice full
will push the world
to one more perigee.
All will stop
and Christ will come -
yet nothing He will stop.
He'll send it on,
the New Year comes.
The living spiral
all moves onward
one more door
to one notch more

§ THE MESAS BELOW GALISTEO

The single car
on 41,
does nothing to these sacred lands -
they tell you of the pioneer
who saw the rocks
as new and future castles,
who saw the light that spread across the desert plain
who say that Coronado
searched, but not in vain.

The valleys here
that drink the fertilizing rain -
the far off pueblos must have seen
as sacred to the Christmastide,
the solstice clouds
dropping water sheets
to spell the mesa bride
and thus declare
the virgin birth.

At Pueblo de San Lazaro
sages know
Elysian Fields, these
escarpments of the gods,
are something that the Earth has set
where spirit, purity, and peace
are met.

§ THE RIO GRANDE AT TAOS

The clear, far sighted.
ever even lands
are like the scent of sage
and wisdom
rooting in the red brown sands.

Below the pines
across the gorge
striated are the ages,
layer cakes of history,
that crumble down
in dusky stones,
tumbling far
to water bulging
past the cliffs
to join the Rio Grande.

At cliff edge
stretching back,
to the blue pastel
of mountain silhouettes,
the rolling desert,
a tawny icing spread upon the cake,
stark in light that filters clear
to lands a mile high.

The pinons sitting there
are living in a peace,
content to be a perfect stand,

an olive green community,

above the cut across the plain -
above the giant trough
that only shows a line
to walkers in the fields,
a sign there is a gorge
where water flows
from north to south New Mexico.

From Taos to the north
beneath the alpine peak,
the desert fields
sweeping here
grow only sage
with twisting roots,
in plant to plant,
band to cluster,
field to ridge,
and ridge to valley,
sage creates its grey blue green.

The wisdom herb,
when crushed,
gives scents that are assigned
to this one place and time:
the Pueblo brave
who looked across the gorge
and knew his gods, his land
thrived here like the pines
that thrill to live atop the cliff
in huddled bands.

MOTIVES OF YOUTH

You bargained for destiny,
like pieces of land,
places ahead
the highway traverses -
and the roads led West.

What law take in hand?
With whom would you go?
What means will you have?
What comes from the quest?

The persons you chose,
the places you went -
alliances joined,
pathways leading
too fast to an end
where no one can see
past the road-bend

and we took the test.
The road signs led West,
but not so far as where day ends -
and never so far as a decade's end, and yet
we chose our best.

BAS-RELIEF

The layers of the limestone cliff
are churned and folded
in an ancient ochre tan
yellowed pelts and brownish sands -
sawed and rounded
formed to heads
that almost are a man

the river may have made them
as it swept and sanded epochs on the stone
or quakes and rain had shook them
when ice in winter chiseled in between them
the layers jumbled to a crowd
of subtle heads and nodules.

They climb the cliff - as generations build
the stuff of histories...
Its faces holding eras
in bas reliefs of hundreds of feet.

that head was a pueblo priest
and that one was a monk
another was a settler
the tilting one - an Indian guide
that upper one a student who died
and countless others -
all made up the culture of the land
the larger book and lesser books
of lives they lived

that took the same amount of shaping -
stories formed at last
in the cutting powers of life

the cliff is staid
in people set in sculpted stone
but the river! Smoky brown and grey
it rushes by and thousands of gallons pass
before the mind can coalesce
a question

Why does it flow so quick
at the foot of the cliff?
Above it the evanescent clouds
form thoughts that shift
and one can a miss a message
looking once away

the present flows so fast
I cannot act in blindness
but run to find the will
of Him who made these elements
so varied -
water, stone, and vapor
divisions of time so different
moments and epochs
seconds or hours
and none is like to where He lives.

but the river... your heart should be glad...
Like the limestone heads in the rock

with stories set in bone
you think that we are done
but the river flows so quick and full
at the foot of the stone

List of Illustrations (photos by John Axline)

(by page)

ii. Mission Santa Barbara
iv. Pacific Grove, Monterey
vi. from Ragged Point, Big Sur
7. oak tree, northern California
9. the University of California, Davis, Music Building
9. cottages across from the Davis train station
11. light house near Ragged Point, Big Sur
15. The Sierras northwest of Bishop
16. Big Sur coast near Santa Lucia
16. the Pacific from San Simeon
19. Pacific sunset from San Simeon
20. Sierras northwest of Lone Pine
20. Mt. Whitney from Lone Pine
24. Mt. Lassen from Hat Creek (cover photo)
24. Mt. Shasta from Antelope
26. Mt. Shasta from Little Shasta church
29. salt flat, from Mohave Preserve, Keno Station
30. Mission Santa Barbara
33. Little Shasta Church, northern California
33. view towards Ventura, Santa Barbara Channel
36. view towards Santa Barbara, Santa Barbara Channel
38. Mojave, California
42. Sunset clouds from Pecos, New Mexico
45. Rain over Cerrillos, from Fort Marcy, Santa Fe
47. The Pecos River north of Pecos
48. Sunset on the Jemez Mountains
50. Turquoise Mountains and Sandia Peak (behind)
53. Sunset at spring equinox over the Jemez Mountains
55. Red mesas at Thoreau

56. The Rio Grande gorge south of Taos
59. Shiprock seen from the Colorado border
61. Tree and rocks over the Pecos River
64. Abobe buildings, Santa Fe

Other Poetry Books by Webster Young:

Cafe Life and Romance (with photos)
Paris and Nice (with photos)

Books by Webster Young:
Music, Painting, and Jung
The Palaces of Music

Poetry Copyright Webster Young 2013-19
Photos Copyright John Axline 2018-19

www.ingramcontent.com/pod-product-compliance
Lightning Source LLC
Chambersburg PA
CBHW061510040426
42450CB00008B/1546